LITTLE ENCYCLOPEDIA OF LACUSTRE MONSTERS

Magnus Olivier

CONTENTS

LITTLE ENCYCLOPEDIA OF LACUSTRE MONSTERS

Magnus Olivier

INTRODUCTION

In the most mysterious and enigmatic corners of the world, lakes hide secrets that awaken the imagination and fuel legends.

Whether beneath the serene waters of majestic lakes or in the shadows of local mythology, lake monsters have captivated human curiosity throughout the centuries.

From the misty waters of Loch Ness to the serene depths of Lake Biwa in Japan, this compendium takes us on a fascinating journey through the mystical waters that have given rise to the world's most captivating legends.

In "Little Encyclopedia of Lake Monsters", we embark on a journey through the sacred waters, dark hiding places and vibrant mythologies that give life to these mysterious creatures.

Each chapter reveals a new story, a new enigma, and immerses us in the richness of cultural beliefs that have influenced the perception of these beings over time.

From legends that have endured generation after generation to contemporary encounters that defy logic, this book invites us to explore the intersection between fantasy and reality in the fascinating world of lake monsters.

Join us on this journey, where deep waters hide secrets that spark the imagination and challenge our conventional understandings of nature.

After a short review of what lake monsters are and are not and the competing theories that we see today, here you will find these mysteries:

Loch Ness Monster (Scotland): Perhaps most famous of all, Nessie, a plesiosaur-like creature, is said to inhabit Loch Ness.

Ogopogo (Canada): Ogopogo is believed to live in Okanagan Lake in British Columbia and is described as a serpentine creature.

Champ (United States/Canada): Associated with Lake Champlain on the US-Canada border, an aquatic being similar to a plesiosaur is reported.

Lagarfljótsorm (Iceland): A sea serpent that supposedly lives in Lake Lagarfljót, known since the Middle Ages.

A monster from the Flathead Lake (United States): Tales of a snake-like monster in Flathead Lake, Montana.

Rivers (South Africa): Said to inhabit rivers and lakes, a crocodile-like creature with tentacles.

Memphre (Canada): Tales of a monster in Lake Memphremagog, described as a snake-like creature.

ARRIVED (Scotland): Supposedly inhabitant of Loch Morar, described as a fish-like creature with snake skin.

Selma (Iceland): A marine worm-like creature that, according to legend, lives in the eastern fjords of Iceland.

Tianchi Lake Monster (China): There is talk of a dragon-like creature in Lake Tianchi, on the border between China and North Korea.

Pillow (United States): Associated with Lake Kussharo in Japan, it is said to be similar to a plesiosaur.

Lariosaur (Italy): A plesiosaur-like creature has been reported in Lake Como.

Van Monster (Turkey): There is talk of a snake-like monster in Lake Van, the largest lake in Turkey.

Legend of Lake Panguipulli (Chile): It is said that a being similar to a giant fish lives in Lake Panguipulli.

Labynkyr Monster (Russia): At Lake Labynkyr, a monster is reported that has been compared to the Scottish Nessie.

Isshii (Japan): Mythical creature associated with Lake Ikeda, described as an octopus-like monster.

Monstruo de Lough Ree (Ireland): In Lough Ree lake, there is talk of a creature similar to a sea horse.

Nahuel Huapi Lake Monster (Argentina-Chile): Legends of a giant fish-like creature in Lake Nahuel Huapi.

Small sausage (Finland): Aquatic being from Finnish mythology, associated with lakes and rivers, known for drowning people.

Muyso (Colombia): In the La Cocha lagoon, there is talk of a creature similar to a giant snake.

Legend of Hoan Kiem Lake (Vietnam): Account of a giant turtle in Hoan Kiem Lake, considered a deity in Vietnamese mythology.

Tota Lake Monster (Colombia): In Lake Tota, an anaconda-like creature is reported.

Mbielu-Mbielu-Mbielu (Congo): Creature from local mythology, sometimes associated with lakes, described as a dinosaur.

Legend of Lake Biwa (Japan): Tales of a snake monster called Oshōgatsu-ujin who lives in Lake Biwa.

LAKE MONSTERS: BETWEEN MYTHOLOGY AND REALITY

In the vast universe of legends surrounding lakes, the fascinating category of lake monsters arises. However, before we delve into the mysterious waters of these narratives, it is essential to understand what constitutes a true lake monster and differentiate it from fantastical or mythological creatures.

What Are Lake Monsters?

Lake monsters are legendary creatures believed to inhabit lakes, reservoirs or bodies of water, and whose existence is often based on folklore stories, local testimonies or anomalous sightings. These creatures, sometimes described as giant snakes, aquatic dragons or unusual shapes, have left an indelible mark on popular culture and have captured the imagination of communities around the world.

Common Characteristics of Lake Monsters:

1. Serpentine or Dragonesque Shape: Many of these monsters are described as having elongated bodies and serpentine shapes, similar to aquatic dragons, reflecting the influence of local mythologies and folklores.

2. Elusive Sightings: Encounters with lake monsters are often brief and elusive, contributing to the mystique that surrounds them. Some legends suggest that these creatures can dive deeply, escaping human gaze.

3. Spiritual or Sacred Connections: In many cultures, lake monsters are linked to spiritual or sacred beliefs. Some communities consider them protective guardians of bodies of water, while others see them as omens.

What Aren't Lake Monsters?

It is crucial to discern between lake monsters and other fantastic creatures that may inhabit legends and mythologies. Some of the key differences include:

1. **Mythological Fantastic Creatures**: While lake monsters may be based on local sightings or popular beliefs, mythological creatures are often derived from deep cultural traditions and may have divine or supernatural properties.

2. **Misunderstood Natural Phenomena**: In some cases, lake monster sightings may be misinterpretations of natural phenomena, such as floating logs, wave patterns, or

conventional aquatic animals.

3. **Fictional Creations**: In the modern era, popular culture has given rise to the creation of fictional lake monsters for entertainment purposes, such as films and novels, which may have no basis in local legends.

In this introductory chapter, we lay the foundation for exploring the intriguing world of lake monsters, remembering that the line between reality and fantasy blurs in the mysterious waters of these aquatic bodies.

BETWEEN MYTHS AND REALITIES: EXPLANATIONS OF THE EXISTENCE OF LAKE MONSTERS

The persistent belief in the existence of lake monsters has led its supporters to offer various explanations that seek to substantiate the presence of these creatures in lakes and bodies of water around the world. Although science often approaches these claims with skepticism, the theories proposed by lake monster enthusiasts offer a fascinating glimpse into how imagination and curiosity have shaped these narratives.

1. Survival of Unknown Species:

One of the most recurring arguments is the possibility that unknown species, not cataloged by conventional science, inhabit the lakes. It is argued that these creatures could be descendants of prehistoric or unknown species, adapted to the lake environment and capable of evading human detection.

Although science has extensively explored the biodiversity of bodies of water, supporters of this theory maintain that there may still be species that remain hidden due to their ability to evade conventional detection methods.

2. Isolated Evolution:

Supporters of the existence of lake monsters suggest that these creatures could have evolved in isolation, adapting to specific conditions of the lake in which they are found. This concept raises the possibility that unique and unknown ecosystems exist deep within some bodies of water.

This theory proposes that these creatures could have adapted to their particular environment, developing specific characteristics that allow them to survive and thrive in a specific ecological niche within the lake.

3. Unknown Dimensions:

More speculative theories suggest that the lakes could act as portals to unknown dimensions, allowing the entry and exit of creatures that do not belong to the conventional plane. This idea, although fantastic, reflects human creativity to explain the inexplicable.

The notion of alternate dimensions or dimensional portals proposes that these creatures could cross between different realities, which would explain their ability to appear and disappear in mysterious ways.

4. Spiritual or Mystical Creatures:

In some cultures, the belief in lake monsters is linked to spiritual or mystical conceptions. It is argued that these creatures are guardians or divine presences that protect bodies of water and give sacred meaning to these environments.

The spiritual creature explanation suggests that the relationship between lake monsters and local communities goes beyond biology and is intertwined with the sacred and the transcendental.

5. Adaptations for Concealment:

The idea that lake monsters have developed adaptations for stealth and concealment is another theory put forward. It is suggested that these creatures may have camouflage abilities or evasive behaviors that allow them to avoid human detection.

This theory explores the possibility that lake monsters have evolved specific strategies to evade human attention, allowing them to remain hidden and escape direct observation.

6. Influence of Popular Culture:

Some supporters argue that the persistence of lake monster stories is due to the influence of popular culture. The continued presence of these creatures in films, books and other media could contribute to the formation of collective perceptions and beliefs.

The idea that media and cultural representations of lake monsters influence public perception highlights how culture and entertainment can shape belief in these creatures.

Scientific Challenges:

Despite these theories, scientists and skeptics highlight the challenges of accepting the existence of lake monsters without solid, verifiable evidence. The lack of conclusive evidence remains a significant obstacle in the scientific acceptance of these creatures.

BETWEEN EVIDENCE AND SKEPTICISM: SCIENTIFIC PERSPECTIVES ON THE NONEXISTENCE OF LAKE MONSTERS

Although belief in lake monsters has endured throughout history, the scientific community tends to approach these claims with skepticism, seeking solid, verifiable evidence before accepting the existence of such creatures. In this chapter, we will explore the scientific perspectives that challenge the idea of the existence of lake monsters and the arguments they present to support their skepticism.

1. Absence of Compelling Evidence:

One of the fundamental arguments presented by scientists is the lack of convincing evidence supporting the existence of lake monsters. Despite decades of anecdotal reports and sightings, the absence of physical and scientifically verifiable evidence makes it difficult to accept these creatures as part of the animal kingdom.

2. Limitations of Current Technology:

Scientists also point out the limitations of current technology to comprehensively explore and study bodies of water. Although sonar and underwater cameras have been used in investigations, the vastness and complexity of the lakes present considerable challenges, making it difficult to obtain conclusive evidence.

3. Alternative Explanations for Sightings:

Skeptics argue that many lake monster sightings can be attributed to more conventional explanations. Elements such as floating logs, light patterns, weather phenomena, and other aquatic animals can create misperceptions and contribute to the creation of myths.

4. Cultural and Psychological Influence:

The influence of culture and human psychology is also highlighted as a contributing factor to the creation and perpetuation of legends about lake monsters. Familiarity with previous stories, suggestion, and a predisposition to believe in the fantastic can influence the interpretation of observed events.

5. Ecological Pressures and Food Availability:

From a scientific point of view, the existence of large unknown creatures in lakes raises questions about the sustainability of such populations. Scientists argue that limited food availability and ecological pressures could make maintaining a population of lake monsters unlikely.

6. Poor Reproducibility of Sightings:

The poor reproduction of documented sightings and the lack of systematic observations make it difficult to scientifically validate claims about lake monsters. The absence of long-term studies and the lack of consistent observations present challenges for scientific evaluation.

LAKE MONSTERS THROUGHOUT HISTORY

Throughout history, lake monsters have had a significant impact on various cultures around the world. Although specific interpretations and stories vary by region, we can identify some general impacts that these aquatic enigmas have had on cultures over time:

1. Element of Mythology and Folklore:

Lake monsters have played a prominent role in the mythology and folklore of many cultures. These creatures are often associated with the creation narrative or local myths that explain natural phenomena.

2. Cultural Identity:

Stories of lake monsters have often become intertwined with the cultural identity of local communities. These creatures become part of the historical narrative and the way a society views and relates to its natural environment.

3. Tourism and Local Economy:

The notoriety of certain lakes and their legends of lake monsters has contributed to tourism in those areas. Local communities often take advantage of these stories to attract visitors, generating income through tourism activities and the sale of related souvenirs.

4. Spiritual Interpretations:

In some cultures, lake monsters have been interpreted as spiritual entities or guardians of sacred bodies of water. These interpretations have influenced local religious practices and rituals.

5. Development of Imagination and Curiosity:

The presence of lake monsters has fueled human imagination and curiosity about the unknown. These stories have encouraged exploration and interest in the fauna and flora of the lakes, as well as ecology in general.

6. Perception of the Natural Environment:

Legends of lake monsters have shaped the perception of bodies of water in popular culture. Lakes, originally seen as mere bodies of water, have been transformed into scenes of mystery and wonder.

7. Element of Moral Teaching:

Some lake monster legends incorporate moral elements or lessons. These stories often convey messages about the importance of respect for nature, caution in the unknown, and the harmonious relationship between humans and their environment.

MYSTERIES IN FILM, MUSIC AND MORE: INFLUENCE OF LAKE MONSTERS ON ARTS AND POPULAR CULTURE

The presence of lake monsters has transcended the waters to immerse itself in the heart of popular culture, leaving a deep mark on various artistic forms. In this chapter, we will explore how these mysterious creatures have influenced film, music, television, literature, and other cultural expressions, revealing their lasting impact on human creativity.

Who:

-       "Loch Ness" (1996): A film that follows the story of a scientist who arrives at Loch Ness to unravel the mysteries surrounding Nessie. This film is just one of many that have used the legend of the Loch Ness

Monster as a backdrop for intriguing narratives.

- "The Water Horse: Legend of the Deep" (2007): Although not directly related to traditional lake monsters, this film features a mythical creature that shares similarities with lake monster legends.

Music:

- Mannheim Steamroller's "Nessie": This New Age music band released a piece of music called "Nessie," which captures the mysterious essence and wonder associated with the Loch Ness Monster.

- "Ogopogo" by The Billy Mitchell Group: A jazz composition inspired by the legend of the Ogopogo, combining musical improvisation with the narrative of the aquatic enigma.

Television:

- "Scooby-Doo and the Loch Ness Monster" (2004): In this special episode of Scooby-Doo, the gang faces mysteries in Scotland, including a visit to Loch Ness and its famous monster.

- "River Monsters" (2009-2017): Although not specifically focused on lake monsters, this television show follows biologist Jeremy Wade as he researches and captures freshwater fish, including some mysterious species.

Literature:

- The Water Horse" by Dick King-Smith: The children's novel that inspired the film of the same name, tells the story of a boy who finds an egg on the beach that turns out to be the offspring of an aquatic monster.

- "The Loch" by Steve Alten: A horror novel that explores the possibility that an ancient monster resides in the depths of Loch Ness, fusing legend with elements of fiction.

Visual art:

- Photograph of Nessie by Marmaduke Wetherell: Although later revealed to be a hoax, the famous photograph of Nessie's neck and head, taken by Marmaduke Wetherell in 1934, became a visual icon associated with the legend of the Loch Ness Monster.

- Paintings and Artistic Representations: Artists around the world have created visual interpretations of lake monsters, from realistic paintings to fantastical illustrations that capture the mysterious essence of these creatures.

Other Cultural Manifestations:

- Themed Festivals and Events: Many regions that have legends of lake monsters hold themed festivals and events that incorporate elements of cultural tradition into activities and entertainment.

- Toys and Merchandising: The image of lake monsters is often reproduced on toys, t-shirts, and other merchandising items, extending the influence of these creatures through cultural consumption.

The influence of lake monsters on arts and popular culture is vast and diverse, manifesting itself in various ways over time. These mysterious creatures continue to inspire human creativity and offer fertile ground for exploring the balance between the unknown and the imagination.

THE LOCH NESS MONSTER

The legend of the Loch Ness Monster, Nessie, has captured the world's imagination and has become an unsolved enigma that endures throughout time. From the earliest stories in Scottish oral tradition to the modern era, the mystery surrounding Nessie continues to be a source of fascination and debate.

History and Mythology:

The legend of the Loch Ness Monster has deep roots in Scottish oral tradition, with stories dating back centuries. However, it was in the modern era that Nessie achieved global fame, becoming a cultural phenomenon.

Physical description:

Nessie is commonly described as a serpentine-looking aquatic creature, with a long, billowing neck that peeks above the surface of the water. Some reports suggest a resemblance to a plesiosaur, a prehistoric marine reptile.

Notorious Sightings:

1. 1933 - The Aldie Mackay Incident: One of the first

notable sightings occurred when Aldie Mackay and his wife reported seeing a dark object moving in the lake while they were driving.

2. 1934 - The Surgeon's Photograph: The famous photograph taken by surgeon Robert Kenneth Wilson shows what appears to be Nessie's neck and head rising out of the water. Although widely known, the authenticity of the image has been the subject of controversy.

3. 1960 - The Tim Dinsdale Recording: Tim Dinsdale filmed a mysterious shape in the lake that moved similar to Nessie's description. His recording has come under extensive scrutiny, but the explanation remains uncertain.

Research and Expeditions:

Over the years, numerous expeditions and studies have been carried out to investigate the alleged presence of Nessie. Teams of scientists and enthusiasts have used advanced technology, such as sonar and underwater cameras, in an effort to find conclusive evidence of the creature's existence.

Theories and Scientific Skepticism:

Although the legend of the Loch Ness Monster has captured the imagination of millions, the scientific community is skeptical. The lack of solid evidence and Nessie's elusive nature have led to many alternative theories. Some suggest that the sightings could be explained by natural phenomena, floating logs or other aquatic animals.

Cultural Impact and Tourism:

Nessie has become an iconic symbol of Scotland and has

left a lasting impact on popular culture. Tourism in the Loch Ness region has flourished, attracting visitors from around the world seeking a glimpse of the famous creature. Souvenirs, books, and exhibitions dedicated to Nessie contribute to the local economy. Although the creature itself remains elusive, the mystery surrounding it has made Loch Ness an unforgettable tourist destination.

5 Curiosities about the Loch Ness Monster:

1. The Name of Nessie: The affectionate nickname "Nessie" for the Loch Ness Monster originated in 1947 in a Scottish newspaper, and has since become the best-known way of referring to the creature.

2. Influence on Pop Culture: Nessie has left an indelible mark on popular culture, appearing in movies, television shows, and being referenced in various forms of entertainment.

3. Underwater Lake Study: In 2019, a team of scientists carried out a comprehensive study of Loch Ness using environmental DNA technology to analyze water samples. Although no evidence of monsters was found, the study revealed valuable information about the lake's aquatic life.

4. Scottish Coin Honoring Nessie: The Bank of Scotland issued a commemorative £1 coin in 2007 featuring Nessie's image, paying tribute to his impact on the region.

5. Nessie Day: In honor of the legendary creature, December 2 is celebrated as Nessie Day, a day to reflect on the fascinating history and mystery surrounding the Loch Ness Monster.

THE OKANAGAN LAKE MONSTER

The legend of Ogopogo, the monster of Okanagan Lake in Canada, has intrigued locals and visitors for generations. This enigmatic aquatic being has been the subject of numerous stories and sightings, making it an emblematic figure of the region.

History and Mythology:

The history of Ogopogo dates back to the legends of the region's First Nations, who told of a mythical creature that lived in the depths of Okanagan Lake. Over time, traditional accounts mixed with modern sightings, giving rise to the contemporary legend of Ogopogo.

Physical description:

Ogopogo is commonly described as a large sea snake, with a series of humps visible above the water surface. Some reports suggest that it has a head similar to that of a horse or other animal, adding an element of diversity to the descriptions.

Notorious Sightings:

1. 1926 - The Mission Beach Incident: One of the first documented sightings occurred when a group of witnesses claimed to have seen a snake-like creature in the waters of Okanagan Lake.

2. 1968 - The Photography of Art Folden: Art Folden captured an image showing a long, dark shape in the lake. Although the photograph is inconclusive, it fueled speculation about the existence of Ogopogo.

3. 2011 - The Richard Huls Video: Richard Huls filmed a video showing a series of ripples and disturbances in the water, which some interpreted as evidence of the presence of Ogopogo.

Research and Expeditions:

Over the years, various investigations and expeditions have been carried out to discover the truth behind Ogopogo. Teams of scientists and enthusiasts have used advanced technology, including sonar and underwater cameras, in an effort to capture conclusive evidence of the creature's existence.

Theories and Scientific Skepticism:

Despite the rich tradition of sightings, the scientific community is skeptical of the existence of Ogopogo. It is suggested that many sightings could be attributed to floating logs, optical illusions or natural lake phenomena.

Cultural Impact and Tourism:

Ogopogo has become an iconic symbol of the Okanagan region and has left a significant mark on local culture. The creature is celebrated through festivals, events and works of art that honor its legendary status. Tourism in the area has flourished thanks to the curiosity around Ogopogo, attracting those seeking a glimpse of the lake monster.

5 Fun Facts about Ogopogo:

1. Varied Name: Before being known as Ogopogo, the creature had different names according to First Nations legends, such as N'ha-a-itk and Naitaka.

2. Historical References: Some believe that Ogopogo has parallels with other sea serpent legends in different cultures around the world.

3. Canadian Coin: In 2011, the Canadian government issued a commemorative 25-cent coin featuring Ogopogo, highlighting its cultural importance.

4. Ogopogo Festival: Every year, the City of Kelowna hosts the "Ogopogo Festival," celebrating the mysterious presence of the creature in the lake.

5. Conservation Hope: Some proponents of the Ogopogo legend believe that the creature's existence could attract attention and interest in the conservation of Okanagan Lake and its surroundings.

CHAMP, THE LAKE CHAMPLAIN MONSTER

The legend of Champ, the Lake Champlain monster, has intrigued residents and visitors to the region that shares the shores of the United States and Canada. From centuries-old tales to modern sightings, Champ has become an enigmatic figure populating the mythology of northeastern America.

History and Mythology:

Champ's history is intertwined with the legends and myths of the indigenous tribes that inhabited the Lake Champlain region. These accounts have persisted over the centuries, merging with more recent sightings and contributing to the legend of Champ.

Physical description:

Champ is commonly described as a being similar to a plesiosaur, with a long neck and a head that rises above the surface of the water. Reports vary as to the creature's exact length and appearance, but the image of a prehistoric being persists in the descriptions.

Notorious Sightings:

1. 1819 - The Sighting of Captain Crum: Captain Crum and his crew claimed to have seen a creature with a long neck while sailing on the lake.

2. 1977 - The Photograph of Sandra Mansi: Sandra Mansi took a photograph showing an elongated shape in the water, which some interpreted as the presence of Champ. The authenticity of the image has been the subject of debate.

3. 2005 - The Dick Affolter Recording: Dick Affolter captured a video showing a series of ripples and disturbances in the water, suggesting the possible presence of a large creature beneath the surface.

Research and Expeditions:

Over the years, various investigations and expeditions have been carried out to unravel the mystery of Champ. Teams of scientists and enthusiasts have used advanced technology, such as sonar and underwater cameras, in an effort to obtain concrete evidence of the creature's existence.

Theories and Scientific Skepticism:

The scientific community has expressed skepticism of Champ's existence, noting that many sightings could be attributed to optical illusions, floating logs or other natural lake phenomena. Although some believe in the possibility of a large unknown animal, the lack of solid evidence has led to doubt.

Cultural Impact and Tourism:

Champ has left a cultural mark on the Lake Champlain region, becoming a symbol of mystery and wonder. The legend has inspired festivals, events and works of art that pay tribute to the possibility of an unknown creature inhabiting the lake's depths.

5 Fun Facts about Champ:

1. The Name Champ: The name "Champ" is an abbreviation of "Champy", an affectionate nickname given to the Lake Champlain monster.

2. Monument Declaration: In 1982, the city of Port Henry, New York, officially declared Champ the "Official Aquatic Creatures Monument."

3. Champ Festival: Every year, the town of Burlington, Vermont, holds the "Champ Festival," where locals and visitors gather to celebrate the legend of the lake monster.

4. Inclusion in Popular Culture: Champ has appeared in books, television shows, and films, contributing to his status as a prominent figure in regional mythology.

5. Unsolved Mystery: Despite sightings and speculation, Champ remains an unsolved mystery, challenging those who venture into the waters of Lake Champlain to discover the truth behind its enigmatic presence.

LAGARFLJÓT SNAKE, LA SERPIENTE DEL LAGO LAGARFLJÓT

The legend of Lagarfljótsormur, the serpent of Lake Lagarfljót in Iceland, delves into the roots of Norse mythology. This legendary creature has left an indelible mark on the region's rich tradition of tales and myths.

History and Mythology:

The story of Lagarfljótsormur is intertwined with Icelandic sagas and myths. The creature is considered a mythical being, and the legends surrounding it have been passed down through generations. The narrative often highlights the duality of the creature as a symbol of the unpredictable nature of the environment.

Physical description:

Lagarfljótsormur is commonly described as a giant snake that lives in the depths of Lake Lagarfljót. According to stories, the creature can grow to astonishing lengths and has the ability to hide among the turbulent waters of the lake.

Notorious Sightings:

1. 1345 - The First Documented Sighting: The first known mention of Lagarfljótsormur dates back to a manuscript from the year 1345, where the creature is described as an elongated snake that wreaked havoc around the lake.

2. 2012 - Hjörtur Kjerúlf's Video: In modern times, Hjörtur Kjerúlf captured a video showing a mysterious shape in the waters of Lake Lagarfljót. Although some interpreted the video as evidence of Lagarfljótsormur, others questioned its authenticity.

Research and Expeditions:

Despite the age of the legend, research and expeditions have been carried out to discover more about Lagarfljótsormur. Modern technology, including sonar and underwater cameras, has been used in an effort to confirm the existence of this mythological creature.

Theories and Scientific Skepticism:

The scientific community generally approaches the legend of Lagarfljótsormur with skepticism, pointing out the lack of conclusive evidence and the possibility that the sightings are misinterpretations of natural phenomena or optical illusions. However, the legend remains an integral part of Icelandic culture.

Cultural Impact and Tourism:

Lagarfljótsormur has left a mark on Icelandic culture and contributed to the mystique of the region. Although it has not achieved the same level of notoriety as some of its counterparts, the lake serpent has been a source of interest and has influenced the cultural narrative of Iceland.

5 Curiosidades about Lagarfljótsormur:

1. Ancestral Legends: Lagarfljótsormur is mentioned in ancient Icelandic sagas, connecting the creature to the cultural and mythological roots of Iceland.

2. The Legend of the Ring: According to an associated legend, Lagarfljótsormur was linked to a magical ring that was buried in the lake. The growth of the creature would be associated with the increase in wealth of whoever owned the ring.

3. Lagarfljót Festival: In some communities near the lake, the "Lagarfljót Festival" is celebrated, where legend and history are intertwined in cultural events and performances.

4. Influence on Art: Lagarfljótsormur has been depicted in various works of art, from paintings to sculptures, as a manifestation of the connection between creativity and mythology.

5. Reflection of Icelandic Nature: The legend of Lagarfljótsormur reflects Iceland's complex relationship with nature, highlighting the coexistence of the mysterious and the everyday in the Icelandic landscape.

THE MONSTER OF FLATHEAD LAKE, MONTANA

The Flathead Lake region of Montana is home to the legend of the Flathead Monster, an enigmatic creature that has captured the imagination of locals and visitors. Over the years, the monster's story has added a touch of mystery to the crystal-clear waters of this stunning lake.

History and Mythology:

The story of the Flathead Lake Monster dates back to the oral traditions of the Native American tribes that have inhabited the region for centuries. These stories have evolved over time, merging with more contemporary tales and contributing to the rich mythology of the area.

Physical description:

Descriptions of the Flathead Lake Monster vary, but it is commonly depicted as a large aquatic creature, with features that suggest similarities to beings such as plesiosaurs. Some reports describe a long neck and a head emerging from the water, while other accounts highlight the presence of a larger, serpentine figure.

Notorious Sightings:

1. 1889 - Fisherman Reports: In the late 19th century, fishermen and locals began sharing stories about encounters with a mysterious creature in Flathead Lake. These initial reports contributed to the legend of the Flathead Monster.

2. 2005 - Helicopter Sighting: In more recent times, a helicopter sighting added a new chapter to the legend. The helicopter's occupants claimed to have seen an unusual shape in the lake's waters, fueling speculation about the monster's existence.

Research and Expeditions:

Over the decades, efforts have been made to investigate the alleged presence of the Flathead Lake Monster. However, the lack of conclusive evidence has kept the existence of this creature a mystery.

Theories and Scientific Skepticism:

The scientific community tends to approach the legend of the Flathead Monster with skepticism, suggesting that the sightings could be attributed to natural phenomena, optical illusions, or even the presence of large fish in the lake. The lack of solid evidence has led some people to consider the possibility that the creature is more of a myth than a biological reality.

Cultural Impact and Tourism:

Although the legend of the Flathead Lake Monster has not achieved the same notoriety as some of its counterparts, it has left its mark on local culture. The story has been passed down through generations, and some local businessmen have capitalized on the mystery to attract curious visitors.

5 Curiosities about the Flathead Lake Monster:

1. Monster Festival: The local community organizes a "Monster Festival" in honor of the legend, with events that celebrate the story and attract enthusiasts and the curious alike.

2. Inspired Art: The Flathead Lake Monster has inspired works of art, from paintings to sculptures, that capture the imagination and intrigue associated with the creature.

3. Influence on Local Pop Culture: Although not as well-known nationally, the Flathead Lake Monster has left its mark on local pop culture, appearing in books and artistic depictions.

4. Evolving Myth: The story of the Flathead Lake Monster has evolved over time, adapting to contemporary culture and maintaining its appeal across generations.

5. Legends of Native Tribes: Native American tribes that have inhabited the region for centuries have their own legends about mystical creatures in the lake, which have influenced the narrative of the Flathead Lake Monster.

MAMLAMBO: THE DEVOURER OF SOULS IN THE WATERS OF SOUTH AFRICA

In the waters of South Africa, the legend of Mamlambo has persisted over the years as a mythical creature with roots in the country's rich cultural tradition. Known as the "Devourer of Souls", Mamlambo adds a touch of mystery to South African folklore narratives.

History and Mythology:

Mamlambo has its roots in Zulu mythology, one of the largest communities in South Africa. According to legends, Mamlambo is an aquatic creature that lives in rivers and lakes, associated with spirituality and mysticism.

Physical description:

Mamlambo's physical description varies in legends, but she is commonly depicted as a serpentine creature with the ability to shapeshift. Some accounts describe a reptilian figure, while others depict it with more humanoid features.

Notorious Sightings:

Unlike some legends of aquatic creatures, Mamlambo is not commonly associated with specific sightings. Instead, their presence manifests itself through mysterious encounters and unusual events, such as unexplained disappearances.

Research and Expeditions:

Given the folkloric nature of Mamlambo and its roots in mythology, there have been no formal scientific investigations or expeditions aimed at discovering evidence of its existence. The creature remains primarily within the domain of cultural beliefs and traditional narratives.

Theories and Scientific Skepticism:

Since Mamlambo is more of a mythological figure than a physical creature, the scientific community generally does not approach its existence from a skeptical point of view. Instead, Mamlambo is considered an expression of the rich oral and mythological tradition of the Zulu region.

Cultural Impact:

Mamlambo has left a lasting mark on Zulu culture and, by extension, the rich cultural diversity of South Africa. The creature serves as a reminder of the connection between spiritual beliefs and nature, providing an element of mystery and wonder in local narratives.

5 Fun Facts about Mamlambo:

1. Soul Eater: Mamlambo is known as the "Soul Eater", and is believed to have the power to influence the lives of those who cross his path.

2. Offerings and Rituals: In Zulu mythology, it is believed that certain rituals and offerings can appease Mamlambo and avoid his wrath.

3. Shapeshifting: Mamlambo's ability to shapeshift adds an element of unpredictability to the legends, as he can appear in a variety of ways.

4. Connection with Night: Mamlambo is commonly associated with night and darkness, adding an aura of mystery to its presence.

5. Oral Transmission: The legend of Mamlambo has been transmitted from generation to generation through oral tradition, highlighting the importance of narrative in the preservation of cultural myths.

MEMPHRE: THE MEANDERING MYSTERY OF CANADA'S WATERS

In the crystalline waters of Lake Memphremagog, in the region of Quebec, Canada, resides the mythical creature known as Memphre. This elusive figure has been part of local narratives for generations, bringing a touch of mystery to the waters it embraces.

History and Mythology:

The legend of Memphre has deep roots in the oral tradition of local communities, especially among the inhabitants of the Memphrémagog region. Over the years, Memphre's story has evolved, fusing cultural beliefs with contemporary tales.

Physical description:

Memphre is commonly described as a serpentine being that dwells in the depths of Lake Memphremagog. Descriptions vary, but the creature is usually depicted as a large snake with a majestic presence and sometimes more fantastical features.

Notorious Sightings:

1. 19th Century - Historical Reports: Reports of sightings of a creature in the waters of Lake Memphremagog date back to the 19th century. Witnesses over the years have claimed to have seen a serpentine figure moving across the surface of the lake.

2. Modern Expeditions: As technology advanced, modern expeditions were undertaken to search for evidence of Memphre's existence. These expeditions used underwater technology and sonar in an effort to document the creature's presence, but the results have been inconclusive.

Research and Expeditions:

Over the years, various investigations and expeditions have been carried out to discover the truth behind the legend of Memphre. However, the creature has proven elusive, and tangible proof of its existence remains elusive.

Theories and Scientific Skepticism:

The scientific community takes a skeptical stance toward the existence of Memphre, citing the lack of conclusive evidence and the possibility of misinterpretations of natural phenomena or sightings of other aquatic animals. Theories vary, with some suggesting that the reports could be attributed to optical illusions or the presence of large fish in the lake.

Cultural Impact and Tourism:

Memphre has left its mark on local culture and contributed to the tourist appeal of the Memphrémagog region. The mythological figure has become a symbol of connection between nature and imagination, attracting curious visitors seeking a fleeting glimpse of this mysterious creature.

5 Fun Facts about Memphre:

1. Lake Inspired Name: The name "Memphre" is derived from Lake Memphremagog, where the creature is believed to live. The choice of name reflects the intimate connection between the legend and local geography.

2. Annual Celebrations: In honor of Memphre, the local community organizes annual events and celebrations that highlight the rich cultural and folklore tradition associated with the creature.

3. Art and Representations: Memphre has been immortalized in various forms of art, from paintings to sculptures, which capture the majesty and mystery attributed to the creature.

4. Legends of Native Tribes: As with many mythological creatures, Memphre has parallels in the legends of the native tribes of the region, demonstrating how cultural narratives are intertwined with local history.

5. Sighting Festivals: Some local events focus on the theme of Memphre sightings, giving visitors the opportunity to explore the legend and participate in the collective fascination surrounding the creature.

MORAG: THE AQUATIC MYSTERY OF SCOTTISH WATERS

In the depths of Loch Morar, in the Scottish lands, resides the mysterious creature known as Morag. This enigmatic figure has been part of local legends, adding a touch of magic and wonder to Scottish folklore narratives.

History and Mythology:

The legend of Morag is rooted in the oral tradition of the local communities surrounding Lake Morar. Over the centuries, the creature has been an integral part of Scottish folklore narratives, merging with the region's rich cultural history.

Physical description:

Morag is commonly described as an aquatic being, similar to a sea monster, that dwells in the depths of Lake Morar. Descriptions vary, but in general, it is attributed with serpentine or plesiosaur-like characteristics, a prehistoric marine reptile.

Notorious Sightings:

1. 19th Century - Historical Reports: Reports of Morag sightings date back to the 19th century, when local witnesses claimed to have seen an unusual creature in the waters of Loch Morar. These reports were documented and contributed to the creation of the legend.

2. Modern Expeditions: As technology advanced, modern expeditions were undertaken to search for evidence of Morag's existence. Despite the efforts, the results have been inconclusive, maintaining the mystery surrounding the creature.

Research and Expeditions:

Over the years, various investigations and expeditions have attempted to uncover the truth behind the legend of Morag. Teams of scientists and enthusiasts have used advanced technology, such as sonar and underwater cameras, in an effort to find conclusive evidence of the creature's existence.

Theories and Scientific Skepticism:

The scientific community adopts a skeptical stance towards the existence of Morag, pointing out the lack of conclusive evidence and the possibility of misinterpretations of natural phenomena or sightings of other aquatic animals. Theories vary, with some suggesting that the reports could be attributed to optical illusions or the presence of large fish in the lake.

Cultural Impact and Tourism:

Morag has left its mark on local culture and contributed to the tourist attraction of the region surrounding Lake Morar. The mythological figure has become a symbol of connection between nature and imagination, attracting curious visitors seeking a fleeting glimpse of this mysterious creature.

5 Fun Facts about Morag:

1. Name Inspired by Lake: The name "Morag" is derived from Lake Morar, where the creature is believed to live. The choice of name reflects the intimate connection between the legend and local geography.

2. Annual Celebrations: In honor of Morag, the local community organizes annual events and celebrations that highlight the rich cultural and folklore tradition associated with the creature.

3. Art and Representations: Morag has been immortalized in various forms of art, from paintings to sculptures, which capture the majesty and mystery attributed to the creature.

4. Legends of Native Tribes: As with many mythological creatures, Morag has parallels in the legends of the native tribes of the region, demonstrating how cultural narratives are intertwined with local history.

5. Sighting Festivals: Some local events focus on the theme of Morag sightings, giving visitors the opportunity to explore the legend and participate in the collective fascination surrounding the creature.

SELMA: THE AQUATIC ENIGMA OF COLD ICELANDIC WATERS

In the icy waters surrounding Iceland, hides an aquatic mystery known as Selma. Part of Icelandic legends, this creature adds a touch of wonder and awe to local narratives.

History and Mythology:

The legend of Selma is woven into Iceland's rich mythological tradition. Through generations, stories of this creature have been passed down orally, merging with Icelandic culture and becoming an integral part of local folklore.

Physical description:

Selma is described as a large aquatic being, often associated with depictions of sea serpents or dragon-like creatures. Its exact appearance varies according to the stories, but the general figure is that of a majestic being that moves through the depths of the ocean that surrounds the island.

Notorious Sightings:

1. Historical Accounts: Reports of Selma sightings date back to historical accounts that have been passed down from generation to generation in Iceland. These accounts often describe close encounters with the creature on the high seas.

2. Modern Observations: Despite the lack of conclusive evidence, there have been modern observations that have fueled the Selma mystery. Witnesses occasionally report seeing something unusual in the surrounding waters, contributing to the persistence of the legend.

Research and Expeditions:

Although research on Selma has been less extensive than in other cases, some enthusiasts and scientists have undertaken expeditions in search of evidence of the existence of this creature. The difficulty of exploring Iceland's cold, remote waters adds an additional challenge to the search.

Theories and Scientific Skepticism:

The scientific community is skeptical about the existence of Selma, pointing out the lack of physical evidence and the possibility of misinterpretations of natural phenomena or sightings of other marine species. Theories vary, with some suggesting that descriptions of Selma could be influenced by myths and legends.

Cultural Impact and Tourism:

Selma has left a mark on Icelandic culture and contributed to the region's tourist appeal. The mythological figure has become a symbol of connection between Iceland's rich tradition and fascination with the unknown, attracting curious visitors who wish to explore the waters surrounding the island.

5 Fun Facts about Selma:

1. Name Inspired by Icelandic Mythology: The name "Selma" has roots in Icelandic mythology and reflects the creature's intimate connection to local legends.

2. Representations in Art: Selma has been depicted in various forms of art, from paintings to sculptures, which capture the majesty and mystery attributed to the creature.

3. Festivals and Celebrations: Some communities in Iceland hold annual festivals and celebrations in honor of Selma, highlighting the cultural importance of the creature in the region.

4. Influence on Literature: The figure of Selma has inspired literary works, poetry and stories, contributing to her status as a literary icon in Icelandic mythology.

5. Maritime Symbolism: Selma is not only a mythological figure, but also a symbol that represents Iceland's unique connection to the ocean and the rich heritage of its maritime legends.

TIANCHI LAKE MONSTER: THE AQUATIC ENIGMA OF THE CHINESE MOUNTAINS

Deep in the majestic Changbai Mountains, on the border between China and North Korea, resides an aquatic enigma known as the Tianchi Lake Monster. This creature, part of the region's rich cultural traditions, adds a touch of mystery to the waters of Lake Tianchi.

History and Mythology:

The legend of the Tianchi Lake Monster is intertwined with the rich history and mythology of China. Over the centuries, folklore narratives have passed down stories of encounters with this mysterious creature at Tianchi Lake, adding an element of wonder to the region.

Physical description:

The Tianchi Lake Monster is described as a large aquatic

creature, often associated with depictions of Chinese dragons. Descriptions vary, but in general, they attribute serpentine characteristics and a majestic presence in the waters of the lake.

Notorious Sightings:

1. Historical Accounts: Reports of sightings of the creature date back to historical accounts that have been part of local legends. Witnesses have claimed to have seen something unusual in the waters of Lake Tianchi, contributing to the mystery surrounding the creature.

2. Folk Narratives: Chinese folk narratives often tell stories of encounters with the Tianchi Lake Monster, highlighting its role in mythology and its connection to traditional culture.

Research and Expeditions:

Although scientific research on the Tianchi Lake Monster has been limited compared to other mysterious creatures, some enthusiasts and scientists have carried out expeditions in an effort to discover the truth behind the legend. The difficulty of exploring the remote mountains and Tianchi Lake adds a unique challenge to the quest.

Theories and Scientific Skepticism:

The scientific community maintains a skeptical stance regarding the existence of the Tianchi Lake Monster, pointing out the lack of conclusive evidence and the possibility of erroneous interpretations of natural phenomena. Theories vary, with some suggesting that the sightings could be explained by the presence of large fish or other natural features.

Cultural Impact and Tourism:

The Tianchi Lake Monster has left its mark on traditional Chinese culture and has contributed to the region's tourist attraction. The mythological figure has become a symbol of connection between nature and China's rich cultural heritage, attracting visitors seeking to explore the mysteries of Lake Tianchi.

5 Curiosities about the Tianchi Lake Monster:

1. Chinese Name: In Chinese, the Tianchi Lake Monster is known as "Chidi Xiaowu" (Akaji   Elementary Schoolblack), which roughly translates to "Little Red Crow of the Lake."

2. Annual Celebrations: Some local communities hold annual celebrations in honor of the Tianchi Lake Monster, highlighting its importance in local culture and traditions.

3. Representations in Art: The figure of the Tianchi Lake Monster has been immortalized in various forms of art, from paintings to sculptures, which capture the majesty and mystery attributed to the creature.

4. Influence on Chinese Literature: The enigma of the Tianchi Lake Monster has inspired literary works in Chinese tradition, demonstrating its impact on literature and cultural narrative.

5. Creature Symbolism: In Chinese mythology, dragons are sacred creatures and symbolize good fortune. The Tianchi Lake Monster's connection to depictions of dragons adds an element of reverence to its mysterious presence.

KUSSIE: THE MYSTERY OF THE ENCHANTED FOREST IN THE UNITED STATES

In the dense forests of the United States, especially in the Appalachian region, a mystery is woven that has baffled those who venture into the wild. Known as the Kussie, this mysterious creature adds a touch of enigma to America's forested landscape.

History and Mythology:

The legend of Kussie has its roots in the oral traditions of the communities that inhabit the forests of Appalachia. Over time, stories of encounters with this creature have formed part of the local folklore narrative, adding an element of intrigue to the natural environment.

Physical description:

Kussie is described as a small, elusive creature, often

associated with the appearance of a goblin-like being. Its exact appearance varies according to the stories, but in general, it is attributed with characteristics that allow it to move easily among the forest vegetation.

Notorious Sightings:

1. Accounts from Local Residents: Residents of the forested areas of Appalachia have shared accounts of Kussie sightings over the years. Witnesses have reported seeing fleeting glimpses of the creature among the trees, but the encounters are brief and elusive.

2. Hiker Encounters: Some hikers and nature lovers have claimed to have had surprising encounters with Kussie while exploring the forests. These encounters are often described as mystical and ephemeral experiences.

Research and Expeditions:

Although Kussie has not been the subject of extensive scientific research, some enthusiasts and curious people have undertaken expeditions in search of clues to the existence of this creature. The elusive nature of Kussie, combined with the vastness of the forests, has made it difficult to obtain conclusive evidence.

Theories and Scientific Skepticism:

The scientific community tends to be skeptical about the existence of creatures like Kussie, pointing out the lack of solid physical evidence. Some suggest that the sightings could be attributed to natural phenomena, such as shadows between trees or active imagination in woodland environments.

Cultural Impact and Tourism:

Kussie has left his mark on local stories and contributed to the cultural connection between the communities that call the Appalachian forests home. Although it has not boosted tourism in the same way as other legends, Kussie remains an integral part of the region's rich folklore tradition.

5 Fun Facts about Kussie:

1. Origins in Appalachian Folklore: Kussie has its roots in the rich folklore of Appalachia, where stories of mysterious beings have been passed down from generation to generation.

2. Guardian of the Forest: In some interpretations, Kussie is considered a guardian of the forest, ensuring natural harmony and the protection of flora and fauna.

3. Comparisons to Other Mythological Creatures: Although unique in its description, Kussie has been compared to other forest-dwelling mythological creatures in different cultures, adding a universal element to its mystery.

4. Inspiration in Regional Art: The figure of Kussie has inspired works of regional art, from paintings to sculptures, that capture the mystical essence of this forest creature.

5. Local Celebrations: Some local communities hold celebrations and festivals that honor the presence of Kussie in their stories and legends, highlighting their importance in local tradition.

LARIOSAURO: AMONG THE MYSTERIOUS WATERS OF LAKE COMO, ITALY

In the serene waters of Italy's picturesque Lake Como, a legend is woven that adds a touch of mystery to the region's natural beauty. The Lariosaur, an enigmatic creature, has been the subject of stories and speculation that dance between reality and fantasy.

History and Mythology:

The legend of the Lariosaur dates back decades, when local residents and visitors began recounting encounters with a mysterious creature in the depths of Lake Como. Local mythology has embraced the idea that this aquatic being adds an element of wonder to the rich history of the region.

Physical description:

The Lariosaur is described as an aquatic creature, similar to a saurian or reptile, that moves nimbly under the surface of Lake Como. Although the descriptions vary, in general, characteristics are attributed to it that evoke the image of an ancient marine reptile.

Notorious Sightings:

1. Historical Accounts: Over time, historical accounts of sightings of the creature in Lake Como have been recorded. Witnesses have reported seeing unusual shapes moving in the waters, which has contributed to the narrative of the Lariosaur.

2. Fishermen's Experiences: Some local fishermen have shared experiences of close encounters with the Lariosaur while carrying out their activities in the lake. These accounts often describe the creature as curious but harmless.

Research and Expeditions:

Although the Lariosaur has not been the subject of extensive scientific research, some enthusiasts and curious people have carried out expeditions in Lake Como in search of evidence of the existence of this creature. The difficulty of exploring the lake's depths has added an element of challenge to the search.

Theories and Scientific Skepticism:

The scientific community adopts a skeptical stance towards the existence of the Lariosaur, pointing out the lack of conclusive physical evidence. Some suggest the sightings could be attributed to natural phenomena, large fish, or other more conventional explanations.

Cultural Impact and Tourism:

The Lariosaur has left a mark on local culture, becoming part of the identity of Lake Como. Although it has not generated mass tourism, the legend of the Lariosaur has added a touch of wonder to the experience of those who visit the region.

5 Curiosities about the Lariosaur:

1. Name Inspired by the Region: The term "Lariosaur" combines the Latin name for Lake Como, "Larius," with the root that suggests the shape of a saurian, creating a name that reflects its connection to the region.

2. Artistic Representations: The figure of the Lariosaur has inspired various artistic representations, from illustrations to sculptures, that capture the mysterious essence of the creature.

3. Local Festivals: In some towns near Lake Como, festivals and events have been held in honor of the Lariosaur, highlighting its importance in regional culture and identity.

4. Influence on Regional Literature: The legend of the Lariosaur has inspired literary works and regional stories that explore the relationship between the creature and life on the shores of Lake Como.

5. Mysteries of the Depths: Although the Lariosaur remains a mystery, its presence has added a sense of awe and wonder to the depths of Lake Como, reminding us that nature still holds secrets to be discovered.

THE MONSTER OF VAN: MYSTERIES IN THE DEPTHS OF LAKE VAN, TÜRKIYE

In the vast waters of Lake Van, Turkey, lies an enigma that has intrigued those seeking to discover the secrets of its depths. The Van Monster, a mysterious creature, has captured the imagination of local residents and those who venture into the region.

History and Mythology:

The legend of the Monster of Van dates back generations, where local communities shared stories about encounters with an unusual creature in the waters of Lake Van. Over time, these narratives have become intertwined with regional mythology, creating an enigma that persists today.

Physical description

The Van Monster is described as a large aquatic creature, with characteristics that have been compared to those of reptiles or sea snakes. Although descriptions vary, in general it is attributed an imposing presence and a serpentine shape.

Notorious Sightings:

1. Historical Accounts: Throughout history, historical accounts of sightings of the Van Monster have been documented. Witnesses have claimed to have seen unusual shapes in the lake's waters, fueling the creature's narrative.

2. Reports from Fishermen: Local fishermen have shared reports of close encounters with the creature while carrying out their activities on the lake. These encounters are often described as fleeting sightings, where the creature dives quickly.

Research and Expeditions:

Although the Van Monster has not been the subject of extensive scientific research, some adventurers and the curious have carried out expeditions into Lake Van to search for evidence of the creature's existence. The difficulty of exploring the depths of the lake has added an element of challenge to these undertakings.

Theories and Scientific Skepticism:

The scientific community maintains a skeptical stance on the existence of the Van Monster, pointing out the lack of conclusive physical evidence. Some theories suggest that the sightings could be explained by natural phenomena, large fish or other elements that generate misinterpretations.

Cultural Impact and Tourism:

Although the Monster of Van has not generated mass tourism, its presence in local mythology has contributed to the cultural identity of the region. The creature remains part of the stories passed down from generation to generation.

5 Curiosities about Van's Monster:

1. Historical References: Some historical references to the creature can be found in ancient texts, where encounters with mysterious aquatic beings in Lake Van are described.

2. Connection to Local Mythology: The Monster of Van is intertwined with local mythology, being an integral part of the beliefs and narratives transmitted by the communities surrounding the lake.

3. Modern Underwater Exploration: Although limited, modern exploration of the depths of Lake Van has used advanced technologies to search for evidence of the creature's existence.

4. Comparisons to Other Cryptids: Like other mysterious creatures in lakes around the world, the Van Monster has been compared to similar myths, generating similarities in stories and legends.

5. Influence on Local Art: The Van Monster has inspired local works of art, from paintings to sculptures, that capture the enigmatic essence of this aquatic creature.

LEGEND OF LAKE PANGUIPULLI: AMONG THE MYSTERIOUS WATERS OF SOUTHERN CHILE

In the heart of the Los Ríos region, in southern Chile, lies the beautiful Lake Panguipulli. However, the calm waters of this lake hide an intriguing legend that has been passed down from generation to generation: the legend of Lake Panguipulli.

History and Mythology:

The legend of Lake Panguipulli has deep roots in the mythology and oral tradition of local Mapuche communities. It is said that a mysterious creature lives in the waters of this lake, a manifestation of the spiritual connection between nature and ancestral beliefs.

Physical description:

The creature associated with the legend of Lake Panguipulli is described as a water serpent or "Cai-Cai Vilu", a mythical entity that, according to Mapuche mythology, can control the waters and their currents. His figure is associated with the strength and power of nature.

Notorious Sightings:

1. Mapuche Stories: Over the years, members of the Mapuche community have shared stories about sightings of the creature in the waters of Lake Panguipulli. These tales are often told with a reverential respect for the aquatic entity.

2. Celebrations and Rituals: The presence of the Cai-Cai Vilu is celebrated in some Mapuche festivities and rituals, highlighting the cultural and spiritual importance that this creature has in local mythology.

Research and Expeditions:

Unlike some other cryptids, Cai-Cai Vilu has not been the subject of modern scientific research or expeditions. Consideration of the creature as part of mythology and spirituality limits conventional scientific exploration.

Local Theories and Beliefs:

The belief in the existence of the Cai-Cai Vilu is, to a large extent, part of the Mapuche worldview. The creature is considered a spiritual being rather than a physical phenomenon, and the relationship between the community and the lake is understood from a more symbolic and spiritual perspective.

Cultural Impact:

The legend of Lake Panguipulli and Cai-Cai Vilu are an integral part of the rich cultural heritage of the region. The connection between the creature and Mapuche spirituality has influenced various artistic manifestations, rituals and celebrations.

5 Curiosities about Cai-Cai Vilu:

1. Spiritual Meaning: The Cai-Cai Vilu is not only a mythological creature; It has a deep spiritual meaning for the Mapuche community, representing the connection between the natural and spiritual world.

2. Oral Transmission: The legend of Cai-Cai Vilu has been transmitted over the centuries through oral tradition, highlighting the importance of narrative in the preservation of cultural beliefs.

3. Art and Crafts: The figure of the Cai-Cai Vilu has inspired works of art and crafts, from paintings to sculptures, that reflect reverence and respect towards this mythical entity.

4. Mapuche Celebrations: Some Mapuche celebrations include rituals in honor of the Cai-Cai Vilu, where they seek to harmonize the relationship between the community and the spiritual creature.

5. Reflection of the Mapuche Worldview: The legend of Lake Panguipulli and Cai-Cai Vilu reflects the Mapuche worldview, which considers nature as a sacred environment full of spiritual beings.

LABYNKYR MONSTER: THE FROZEN ENIGMA OF THE SIBERIAN DEPTHS, RUSSIA

In the icy waters of Siberia, Russia, lies a mysterious lake known as Labynkyr. In local legends, this lake is said to be home to an enigmatic creature that has captured the imagination of those who explore its remote shores. Welcome to the riddle of the Monster of Labynkyr.

History and Mythology:

The story of the Labynkyr Monster is mixed with local narratives and oral traditions of Siberia. The legend has been passed down from generation to generation, fueling fascination with the mysterious inhabitant of the lake's dark depths.

Physical description:

The physical description of the Monster of Labynkyr varies

according to local accounts. Some describe it as a reptile-like creature, while others suggest it could be a plesiosaur or even a Siberian variant of the famous Loch Ness monster.

Notorious Sightings:

1. Fishermen's Tales: Local fishermen have shared stories about close encounters with an unknown creature in Lake Labynkyr. Reports often mention unusual movements in the water and mysterious shadows lurking in the depths.

2. Scientific Expeditions: Although not as well known as other cryptids, Labynkyr has attracted the attention of scientific expeditions. Although these expeditions primarily seek data on the climate and geology of the area, they sometimes include observations of local fauna.

Research and Expeditions:

Research on the Labynkyr Monster is scarce compared to other cryptids. The inaccessibility of the area and extreme weather conditions have limited efforts to thoroughly study the lake and its possible inhabitant.

Theories and Scientific Skepticism:

Given the lack of solid evidence and clear observations, the scientific community is skeptical about the existence of the Labynkyr Monster. It is suggested that many sightings could be attributed to natural phenomena or misinterpretations of the local fauna.

Cultural Impact:

Although the legend of the Labynkyr Monster has not had as wide a cultural impact as some other mysterious creatures, it remains part of Siberia's rich lore and contributes to the sense of mystery surrounding the region.

5 Curiosities about the Labynkyr Monster:

1. Unexplored Lake: Labynkyr is known to be one of the most unexplored and least accessible lakes in Siberia, adding an aura of mystery to any story associated with it.

2. Extreme Climate: The region surrounding Labynkyr experiences extreme weather conditions, with long, cold winters. This has made detailed investigations and explorations difficult.

3. Comparisons to Other Cryptids: Like other mysterious lakes in the world, Labynkyr is sometimes compared to similar creatures, suggesting that certain myths share cultural patterns.

4. Local Legends: Local inhabitants have incorporated the legend of the Labynkyr Monster into their folklore, creating a connection between the creature and the cultural identity of the region.

5. Challenges to Research: Logistical difficulty and extreme weather conditions have been significant challenges to any attempt at comprehensive scientific research around Labynkyr.

ISSHII: THE TROUBLED WATERS OF MYSTERY IN JAPAN

In the tumultuous waters of Japanese mythology lies a fascinating mystery: Isshii, a creature that has emerged from local narratives to intrigue and baffle those who search for answers in the depths of Japan.

History and Mythology:

Isshii has its roots in rich Japanese mythology, where mystical creatures often coexist with gods and spiritual beings. Although less known than some of his legendary peers, Isshii has left his mark on Japan's folklore.

Physical description:

Isshii's physical description varies according to legend, but he is commonly depicted as a large aquatic serpent with mystical properties. Some stories suggest that it can change shape, adapting to the waters it inhabits.

Notorious Sightings:

1. Historical Accounts: Over the centuries, accounts of sightings of Isshii-like creatures in different bodies of water in Japan have been recorded. These stories are often intertwined with the country's rich spiritual tradition.

2. Artistic Representations: Isshii has been depicted in various artistic works, from ancient scrolls to contemporary illustrations. These depictions often capture the majesty and enigmatic nature of the creature.

Research and Expeditions:

Unlike some cryptids that have attracted scientific attention, specific research on Isshii is limited. Stories and sightings have been passed down primarily through oral tradition and cultural representations.

Theories and Skepticism:

Given Isshii's mythical context in Japanese mythology, conventional scientific theories do not apply in the same way as they would with real biological creatures. Scientific skepticism is based on the understanding that Isshii could be more of a symbolic manifestation than a physical creature.

Cultural Impact:

Isshii's presence has left a lasting mark on Japanese culture. The creature has been integrated into various forms of artistic expression and has influenced the perception of water as an element full of mystery and spirituality.

5 Fun Facts about Isshii:

1. Link with Aquatic Deities: In some legends, Isshii is associated with Japanese aquatic deities, emphasizing his connection with the spiritual realm of water.

2. Regional Variants: Throughout Japan, different regions may have variations in Isshii's history and appearance, highlighting the cultural diversity in the perception of the creature.

3. Artistic Inspiration: Isshii has been a constant source of inspiration for Japanese artists throughout the centuries, appearing in paintings, prints and other forms of visual expression.

4. Rituals and Festivals: Some communities have developed rituals and festivals in honor of Isshii, recognizing his role in local mythology and seeking the protection of the waters.

5. Adaptation in Pop Culture: Although less known worldwide than some Western cryptids, Isshii has found his place in Japanese pop culture, appearing in films, anime and other forms of entertainment.

LOUGH REE MONSTER: INTO THE MISTS OF IRISH WATERS

In the misty waters of Ireland, specifically Lough Ree Lake, lies an aquatic enigma that has intrigued locals for generations: the Lough Ree Monster. This mysterious inhabitant has woven his own legend into local narratives and has left his mark on the rich folklore tradition of the Emerald Isle.

History and Mythology:

The story of the Lough Ree Monster is intertwined with rich Irish mythology and folklore. Over the years, stories have been passed down from generation to generation, fueling fascination with the lake's mysterious inhabitant.

Physical description:

Physical descriptions of the Lough Ree Monster vary, but it is commonly depicted as a large aquatic creature, similar to a wriggling sea monster. Local narratives often highlight their elusive nature and ability to disappear into the lake's deep waters.

Notorious Sightings:

1. Historical Accounts: Throughout history, numerous accounts of sightings of the Lough Ree Monster have been recorded. These accounts often come from fishermen and locals who have witnessed the creature's presence in the calm waters of the lake.

2. Local Stories: The communities surrounding Lough Ree have incorporated the presence of the monster into their local stories and legends. These stories are often passed down as an integral part of the region's cultural identity.

Research and Expeditions:

Although the Lough Ree Monster has not attracted the same scientific attention as some better-known cryptids, stories and sightings have sparked the interest of local researchers and paranormal enthusiasts.

Theories and Skepticism:

The scientific community generally takes a skeptical stance towards the existence of the Lough Ree Monster. Conventional explanations suggest that the sightings could be attributed to natural phenomena, optical illusions, or even the rich imaginations of those who have shared the stories.

Cultural Impact:

The presence of the Lough Ree Monster has left a mark

on local culture and the perception of the lake itself. The creature has become a prominent feature of oral histories and has contributed to the creation of a unique identity for the community that lives nearby.

5 Curiosities about the Lough Ree Monster:

1. Artistic Inspiration: The Lough Ree Monster has been a source of inspiration for local artists, appearing in works of art, poems and other creative expressions.

2. Annual Celebration: Some communities around Lough Ree have instituted annual celebrations honoring the presence of the monster, often including cultural and recreational events.

3. Local Tourism: Despite uncertainty over the monster's real existence, Lough Ree has seen an increase in local tourism related to the legend.

4. Associated Legends: Stories of the Lough Ree Monster are sometimes intertwined with other Irish legends and tales, further enriching the tapestry of local mythology.

5. Contribution to Orality: The legend of the monster has contributed to the oral tradition of the region, serving as a reminder of the human capacity to weave fascinating narratives even in everyday natural environments.

NAHUEL HUAPI LAKE MONSTER: AMONG THE PATAGONIAN MOUNTAINS

Among the majestic mountains of Argentine and Chilean Patagonia, in the waters of Lake Nahuel Huapi, hides an aquatic mystery that has captivated locals and adventurers alike: the Lake Nahuel Huapi Monster. This enigmatic creature has woven its own legend into the region's rich lore, contributing to the fascination with the secrets that lie in the lake's depths.

History and Mythology:

The history of the Nahuel Huapi Lake Monster is intertwined with the cultural roots of Patagonia. Indigenous narratives and local legends have shaped the perception of this mysterious creature over time.

Physical description:

The physical description of the Nahuel Huapi Lake Monster varies in stories, but it is commonly represented as a large aquatic creature with a serpentine body. Popular imagination has suggested similarities with classical depictions of aquatic monsters.

Notorious Sightings:

1. Indigenous Stories: The indigenous communities of the region have shared stories about the presence of the monster long before the arrival of European colonizers. These stories often include warnings and respect for the creature.

2. Modern Testimonies: Throughout the 20th century and in the contemporary era, there have been testimonies of sightings of the Nahuel Huapi Lake Monster. Some reports come from fishermen and local residents who claim to have seen the creature briefly emerging from the depths.

Research and Expeditions:

Although the Nahuel Huapi Lake Monster has not been the subject of intensive scientific research, curiosity and interest in the creature has led to organized expeditions and searches. Teams of researchers and enthusiasts have attempted to document and understand the monster's presence in the lake.

Theories and Skepticism:

Given the lack of solid scientific evidence, the academic community generally takes a skeptical stance towards the existence of the Nahuel Huapi Lake Monster. Conventional theories suggest that the sightings could be attributed to natural phenomena or misinterpretations of floating objects in the water.

Cultural Impact:

The presence of the Nahuel Huapi Lake Monster has left an indelible mark on the culture of Patagonia. The creature has become part of the local identity and has contributed to the region's rich tradition of myths and legends.

5 Curiosities about the Nahuel Huapi Lake Monster:

1. Name Mapudungun: In indigenous traditions, the monster is often referred to by the Mapudungun name "The Leather", a mythical creature related to the waters.

2. Influence on Regional Art: The Nahuel Huapi Lake Monster has inspired various artistic manifestations, from paintings to sculptures, contributing to the cultural expression of the region.

3. Annual Celebration: Some communities around Lake Nahuel Huapi have instituted annual celebrations that honor the presence of the monster, fusing tradition with festive events.

4. Warning Myths: In indigenous stories, the Nahuel Huapi Lake Monster is often associated with warnings and respect for the waters, serving as a mythical figure that teaches lessons of caution.

5. Tourist Attraction: Despite doubts about the real existence of the monster, Lake Nahuel Huapi has experienced an increase in tourism, with visitors seeking not only the natural beauties, but also the mystery that surrounds the lake.

NÄKKI: THE AQUATIC ENIGMA OF FINNISH WATERS

In the mythological waters of Finland, an aquatic enigma has persisted throughout the centuries: Näkki. This mythical creature has left a mark on Finnish legends, being a figure that combines fascination and caution in the rich tradition of Nordic folklore.

History and Mythology:

Näkki's story is intertwined with the roots of Finnish folklore. Described as an aquatic being, Näkki has been part of the stories told along the lakes and rivers of Finland, passed down from generation to generation.

Physical description:

The physical representation of Näkki varies across traditions, but he is commonly described as an aquatic creature with the ability to shapeshift. It can take on the appearance of an attractive being to attract its victims.

Encounter Stories:

1. Deception and Stealth: Näkki's stories often warn of his ability to deceive the unsuspecting. He can appear as a charming being to attract those who approach the waters, only revealing his true nature when it is too late.

2. Guardian of the Waters: Some narratives present Näkki as a guardian of the waters, with the ability to punish those who show disrespect towards bodies of water.

Beliefs and Rituals:

Näkki's presence has influenced local beliefs and rituals. Practices have been developed to appease or avoid Näkki, including offerings on the banks of lakes and the observance of certain behaviors when approaching water.

Cultural Impact:

Näkki has left its mark on Finnish culture, becoming a fascinating component of local folklore. Their story has been told in various forms, from oral accounts to modern adaptations in literature and art.

5 Fun Facts about Näkki:

1. Traditional Offerings: In some regions of Finland, traditional offerings to Näkki include food and valuable items that are left on the banks of bodies of water as a sign of respect and caution.

2. Local Festivals: Some communities celebrate local festivals that pay tribute to Näkki, incorporating theatrical performances and ceremonies to remember the importance of respect for the waters.

3. Shape Changing: Näkki is known for his ability to change

shape, adapting to circumstances to attract those who venture near water.

4. Warning Symbolism: The figure of Näkki serves as a warning symbol in Finnish stories, teaching lessons about the importance of caution and respect for nature.

5. Influence on Art: Näkki has inspired various artistic expressions in Finland, from paintings to music, serving as a source of creativity in the representation of local mythology.

MUYSO: THE MYSTERIOUS CREATURE OF COLOMBIAN WATERS

In Colombian waters, among the rivers and lakes that meander through the country, there is an aquatic enigma that has intrigued local communities: Muyso. This mysterious creature, part of the rich Colombian folklore tradition, has captured the imagination and respect of those who have woven their lives with the waters that house this enigmatic figure.

History and Mythology:

Muyso's story is intertwined with the mythical narratives of Colombia's indigenous and Afro-descendant cultures. It is considered an aquatic creature with unique characteristics that give it a special place in local legends.

Physical description:

Muyso is commonly described as a serpentine creature, similar to a snake or anaconda, but with unique attributes. Some depictions include fantastical elements, such as horns or glowing scales.

Encounter Stories:

1. Guardian of the Waters: Muyso is often considered a guardian of the waters, protecting bodies of water and punishing those who show disrespect or recklessness near them.

2. Night Encounters: Stories about encounters with Muyso often occur in the darkness of the night, contributing to the aura of mystery that surrounds this creature.

Beliefs and Rituals:

The communities that share the presence of Muyso have developed specific beliefs and rituals. Some make symbolic offerings or avoid certain behaviors near bodies of water as a sign of respect for the creature.

Cultural Impact:

Muyso has become deeply integrated into Colombian culture, becoming a key component of local legends. The creature has inspired not only oral histories, but also artistic expressions that reflect the connection between mythology and cultural identity.

5 Fun Facts about Muyso:

1. Regional Variants: Representations of Muyso may vary in different regions of Colombia, adapting to local beliefs and

experiences.

2. Cultural Syncretism: Muyso is often part of a cultural syncretism, fusing elements of indigenous beliefs with Afro-descendant and European influences.

3. Influence on Music: The figure of Muyso has inspired musical compositions, fusing oral tradition with contemporary artistic expressions.

4. Local Celebrations: In some communities, local celebrations are held in honor of Muyso, including rituals, music and dance that reflect the rich cultural diversity of Colombia.

5. Message of Environmental Respect: The legend of Muyso carries with it a message rooted in respect for nature and its wonders, serving as a cultural guide for harmonious coexistence with the environment.

HOAN KIEM LAKE: WHERE THE VIETNAMESE LEGEND LIES

In the serene waters of Hoan Kiem Lake in Vietnam, lies a legend that has endured throughout the centuries, fusing history, spirituality and mystique. In this chapter, we will explore the fascinating history surrounding this lake, where reality and fantasy are intertwined in rich Vietnamese tradition.

History and Mythology:

The legend of Hoan Kiem Lake dates back to the 15th century, during the reign of Le Loi, a Vietnamese national hero. The story tells of Le Loi's encounter with a giant turtle, marking the beginning of a unique connection between historical reality and the mystical essence of the lake.

Physical description:

In the center of the lake, Jade Island (Dao Ngoc) is home to the Ngoc Son Temple, a sacred site that has played a crucial role in the legend of Hoan Kiem Lake. The giant turtle, known as the Golden Lake Turtle, is a central figure in the narrative.

The Legend of the Golden Turtle:

1. Le Loi and the Celestial Sword: Legend has it that Le Loi received a celestial sword that helped him lead the resistance against the Chinese invaders. After the victory, a golden turtle emerged from the lake and claimed the sword, returning it to the gods.

2. Symbol of Spirituality: The Golden Turtle is considered a symbol of spirituality and connection with the gods in Vietnamese mythology. Its presence in the lake adds a sacred dimension to the environment.

Beliefs and Rituals:

The legend of Hoan Kiem Lake has influenced local beliefs and rituals. The Ngoc Son Temple attracts devotees and visitors, who perform rituals and offerings in honor of the Golden Turtle and Le Loi.

Cultural Impact:

Hoan Kiem Lake and its legend are fundamental elements in Vietnamese culture. In addition to their spiritual importance, the lake and the turtle have become national symbols that evoke a deep sense of identity and pride.

5 Curiosities about Hoan Kiem Lake:

1. Ngoc Son Temple: Ngoc Son Temple, located on Jade

Island, pays homage to the Golden Turtle and is an important sacred and tourist destination.

2. Annual Rituals: Annual rituals are held at Ngoc Son Temple to commemorate Le Loi's victory and honor the Golden Turtle.

3. Endangered: Although legend mentions a golden turtle, the lake has been home to an endangered species of turtle known as the Rafetus Turtle.

4. Ngoc Son Poem: At Ngoc Son Temple, a poem engraved on a stone commemorates the legend, adding a poetic touch to the experience.

5. National Symbol: The image of Hoan Kiem Lake, with its Jade Island and the Golden Turtle, has become a national symbol of Vietnam, capturing the imagination of its people and visitors.

LAKE TOTA MONSTER: BETWEEN COLOMBIAN WATERS AND ANDEAN LEGENDS

In the depths of Lake Tota, the largest lake in Colombia, hides a legend that has been transmitted through generations. The Lake Tota Monster emerges from the waters as a fascinating enigma that fuses the rich Andean tradition with the exploration of the natural mysteries of Colombia.

History and Mythology:

The legend of the Lake Tota Monster has its roots in the Andean worldview and indigenous narratives of the region. Mystical properties are attributed to it and it is often linked to natural events and unexplained phenomena in the lake.

Physical description:

The figure of the Lake Tota Monster varies in descriptions, but it is commonly associated with a large aquatic creature, similar to a snake or fish, that moves in the depths of the lake.

Local Legends:

1. Guardian of Water: In some legends, the Lake Tota Monster is considered a guardian of water, ensuring the purity and harmony of the lake.

2. Interactions with Anglers: Stories are told of anglers who have had unusual encounters with the creature, from distant sightings to closer encounters that defy explanation.

Beliefs and Rituals:

The communities surrounding Lake Tota have woven the legend of the monster into their beliefs and rituals. Some make symbolic offerings to ensure the protection and balance of the lake.

Cultural Impact:

The Lake Tota Monster is not only an element of local mythology, but has also left its mark on Colombian culture, serving as a reminder of the connection between nature and the stories that surround it.

5 Curiosities about the Lake Tota Monster:

1. Lake of Glacial Origin: Lake Tota is of glacial origin and is

located at a considerable altitude in the Andean mountain range, which adds a mystical air to its surroundings.

2. Change in Water Color: Changes in the color of the lake's water have been recorded, attributed to natural phenomena and sometimes associated with the activity of the Lake Tota Monster.

3. Contemporary Sightings: Although legends have endured, contemporary sightings of the Lake Tota Monster are rare and often face skepticism.

4. Natural Heritage: Lake Tota and its legend contribute to the natural and cultural heritage of Colombia, attracting visitors who seek to explore both the beauty of the lake and the stories that surround it.

5. Reflection of the Andean Worldview: The legend of the Lake Tota Monster reflects the Andean worldview, where nature and the spiritual are intertwined, creating a narrative rich in symbolism.

MBIELU-MBIELU-MBIELU: IN THE DEPTHS OF THE CONGO JUNGLE

In the lush jungles of the Congo, a mystery is woven between the dense vegetation and rich biodiversity. The creature known as Mbielu-Mbielu-Mbielu emerges from local mythology and the narratives of indigenous populations, adding a touch of enigma to the natural wonders of the Congo.

History and Mythology:

Mbielu-Mbielu-Mbielu is a figure in Congo mythology, especially among local tribes. Its name translates as "animal that looks like an animal but also like another animal," reflecting its elusive and unique nature.

Physical description:

Descriptions of Mbielu-Mbielu-Mbielu vary, but it is commonly attributed with characteristics that defy conventional categorizations. It is said to have features of different animals, creating a mystical image that is difficult to define.

Local Legends:

1. Guardian of the Jungle: Mbielu-Mbielu-Mbielu is often considered a guardian of the jungle, representing the connection between nature and local communities.

2. Elusive Encounters: Legends tell of elusive encounters with the creature, where it vanishes into the undergrowth before a clear view can be obtained.

Beliefs and Rituals:

The figure of Mbielu-Mbielu-Mbielu is intertwined with the beliefs of local communities about the importance of respecting and preserving the forest. Rituals are performed to honor the creature and promote harmony with the natural environment.

Cultural Impact:

Mbielu-Mbielu-Mbielu is not only part of local mythology, but also influences the communities' relationship with the forest and biodiversity. The creature becomes a reminder of the need to preserve ecosystems.

5 Fun Facts about Mbielu-Mbielu-Mbielu:

1. Rich Ecosystem: The Congo region, where Mbielu-Mbielu-Mbielu is located, is home to one of the richest biodiversity rainforests in the world.

2. Connection with the Okapi: Some legends suggest that Mbielu-Mbielu-Mbielu could have a connection with the

okapi, a relative of the giraffe that lives in the same region.

3. Indigenous Testimonies: Testimonies of Mbielu-Mbielu-Mbielu sightings come mainly from indigenous communities, contributing to the richness of local mythology.

4. Challenge to Science: The elusive nature of Mbielu-Mbielu-Mbielu has presented a challenge to science, which struggles to understand and document the creature conclusively.

5. Congo Conservation: The legend of Mbielu-Mbielu-Mbielu serves as a symbolic reminder of the importance of conservation in the Congo, highlighting the need to protect the rainforest and its biodiversity.

LEGEND OF LAKE BIWA: IN THE SACRED WATERS OF JAPAN

In the land of the rising sun, Japan, the waters of Lake Biwa shelter a legend that fuses the spiritual with the natural. The mysterious creature that lurks in its depths adds a touch of enigma to the rich Japanese mythology, turning Lake Biwa into a scene of wonders and mysteries.

History and Mythology:

The Legend of Lake Biwa dates back centuries, rooted in Japanese spiritual tradition. The lake, the largest in Japan, is considered sacred and has inspired tales of mystical beings who reside in its waters.

Physical description:

The Lake Biwa creature is known for its serpentine appearance, with glistening scales moving through the waters. It is believed to have spiritual properties and is linked to the gods of Shintoism.

Local Legends:

1. Guardian of the Lake: The creature of Lake Biwa is considered a spiritual guardian, ensuring harmony between the earthly and divine worlds.

2. Mystical Encounters: Stories are told of mystical encounters with the creature, where those who have been blessed with its presence have experienced fortune and divine protection.

Beliefs and Rituals:

The communities surrounding Lake Biwa have integrated the legend into their beliefs and rituals. Ceremonies are held to honor the creature and preserve the sacredness of the lake.

Cultural Impact:

The Legend of Lake Biwa has left a deep impression on Japanese culture, influencing the way society perceives the connection between the natural and the spiritual. The creature has become a symbol of respect for nature.

5 Curiosities about the Legend of Lake Biwa:

1. Influence on Art: The legend of Lake Biwa has inspired numerous Japanese works of art, from prints to paintings, capturing the magic of the lake and its creature.

2. Spiritual Pilgrimages: Lake Biwa attracts pilgrims and believers who seek blessing and spiritual connection with the mystical creature.

3. Festivals in Honor of the Lake: Annual festivals are held

in honor of Lake Biwa, where communities participate in rituals and activities to maintain harmony with nature.

4. Lake of Biodiversity: In addition to legend, Lake Biwa is known for its unique biodiversity, hosting endemic species that contribute to its ecological importance.

5. Reflection of Japanese Spirituality: The legend reflects the deep spirituality of the Japanese people and their respect for nature, creating a narrative that transcends the earthly.

www.ingramcontent.com/pod-product-compliance
Lightning Source LLC
Chambersburg PA
CBHW070819280726